The CHRISTMAS LIZARD

PRESENTED TO

FROM

DATE

HONOR BOOKS
Tulsa, Oklahoma

A special thanks to God for those divine moments when stories are born...

To Mom and Dad for raising such a curious boy...

And to Mr. Hammock, who showed me that lizards can do anything.

The Christmas Lizard

2nd Printing

ISBN 1-56292-619-5
Copyright © 2000 by Blue Yonder Films

 Published by Honor Books
P.O. Box 55388,
Tulsa, Oklahoma 74155

Charlie loved all kinds of pets,
from shaggy dogs to sleepy cats.
What should he get?

A slippery fish or spotted frog?

A parakeet or pollywog?

No.
Charlie wanted something different for Christmas.

A lizard!

What a Christmas present—
 a squiggly, scaly,
green iguana.

Charlie fed him lettuce, broccoli,
and strawberries . . . and named
him Oscar.

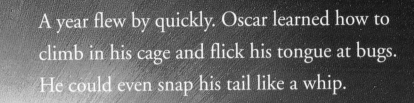

A year flew by quickly. Oscar learned how to climb in his cage and flick his tongue at bugs. He could even snap his tail like a whip.

As winter winds rattled the windows, Oscar noticed a change around the house. Charlie and his mom and dad sang songs. They hung red and green decorations all around the house— even on his cage! *What's going on?* Oscar wondered. *I wish I could find out!*

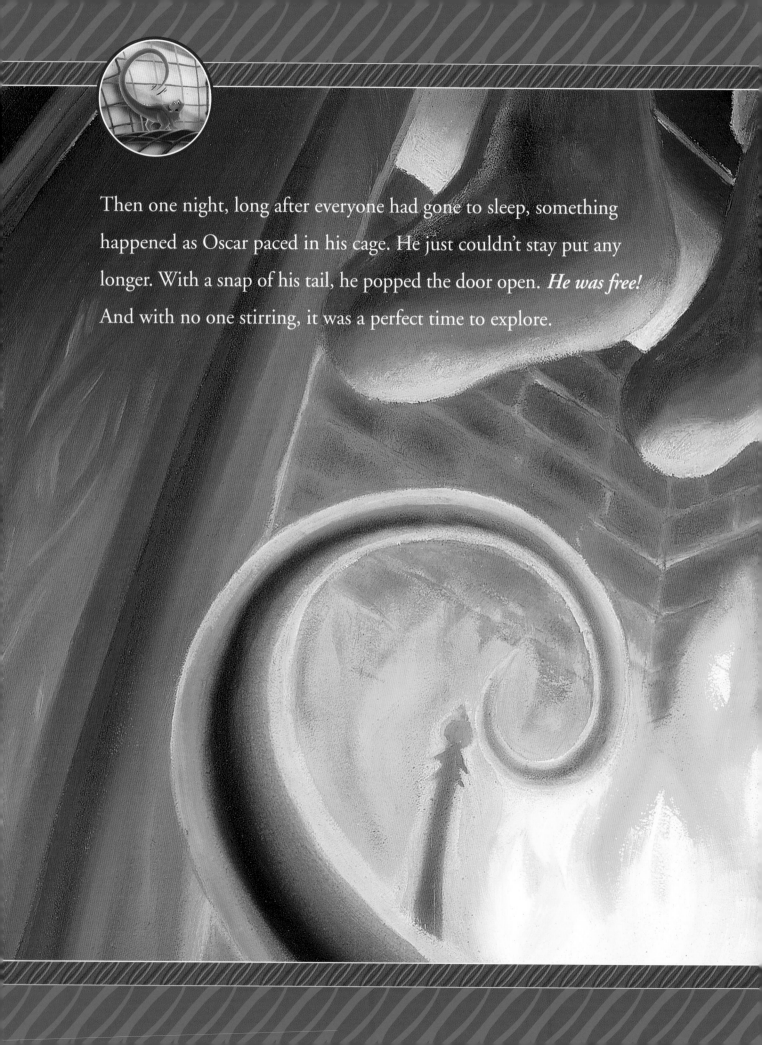

Then one night, long after everyone had gone to sleep, something happened as Oscar paced in his cage. He just couldn't stay put any longer. With a snap of his tail, he popped the door open. *He was free!* And with no one stirring, it was a perfect time to explore.

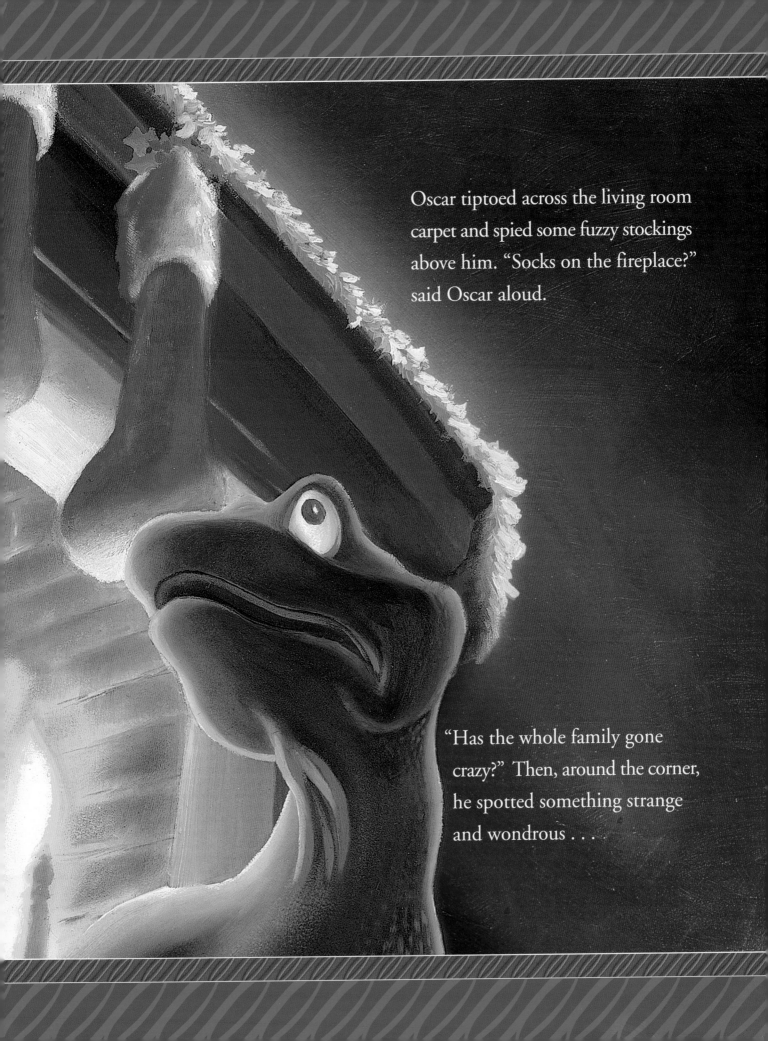

Oscar tiptoed across the living room carpet and spied some fuzzy stockings above him. "Socks on the fireplace?" said Oscar aloud.

"Has the whole family gone crazy?" Then, around the corner, he spotted something strange and wondrous . . .

. . . a tree.

And not just any tree. What a glittering display!
The tree branches sparkled with colored glass balls,
bright decorations, and tiny lights. "How on earth
did a tree grow in the living room?"

The tree stretched all the way to the ceiling. Could he climb all the way to the top? He had to find out. On tiptoe, he finally reached the bottom branches. So up he went. Up and up. Around and around. Higher and higher and around and around.

Soon it seemed as if Oscar wasn't in a tree at all but a dark and winding forest. Then around the next turn, he discovered he was not alone.

"*Halt!*" said a gruff voice. It was the Nutcracker, one of the largest ornaments on the tree. He wore his giant, jagged beard with pride and spoke in a Russian accent. "Who goes climbing at this hour?"

"I'm sorry," said Oscar. "I didn't know this tree was yours."

"It isn't, young comrade," the Nutcracker chuckled. "A Christmas tree is for everyone!"

"Christmas?" Oscar's eyes widened. "I've heard of that. But what is it?"

The Nutcracker laughed. "Why, it's the biggest celebration of the year! There are always parties and music and lots and lots of food!"

"A party? For what?" Oscar asked.

"For goodwill, peace on earth, that sort of thing. I'll show you!"

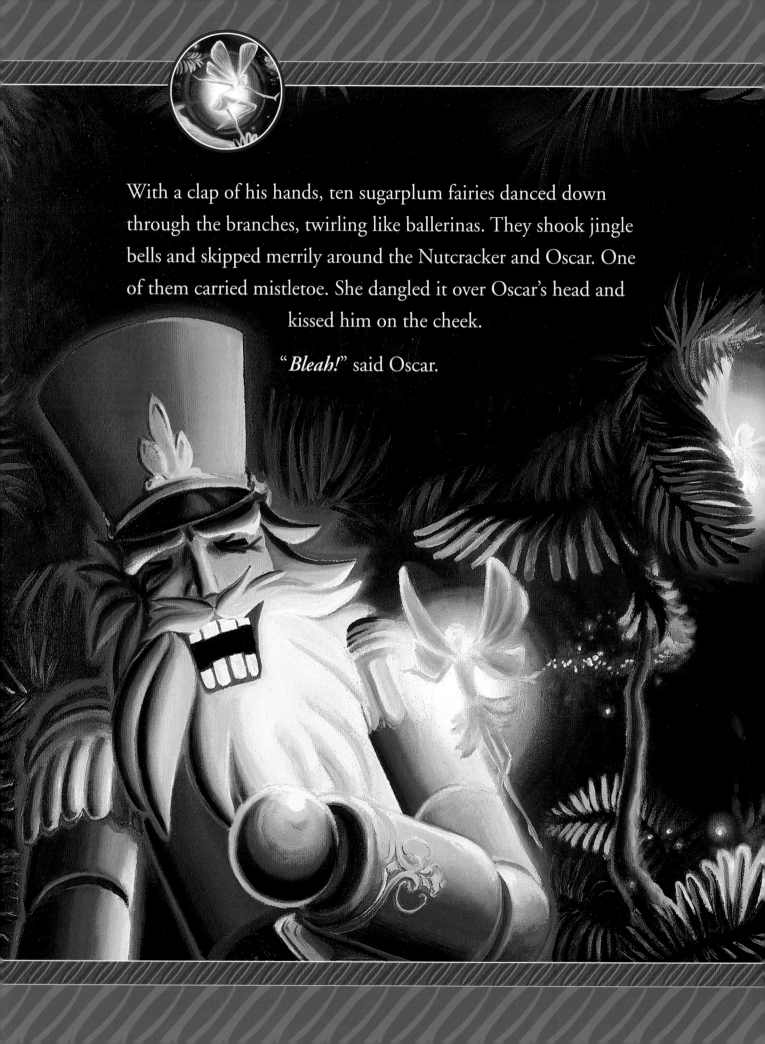

With a clap of his hands, ten sugarplum fairies danced down through the branches, twirling like ballerinas. They shook jingle bells and skipped merrily around the Nutcracker and Oscar. One of them carried mistletoe. She dangled it over Oscar's head and kissed him on the cheek.

"*Bleah!*" said Oscar.

Giggling, they danced out of sight.

"So that's what Christmas is?" asked Oscar.

"Pretty much, comrade," said the Nutcracker. "And you'd best be careful if you climb any higher. A Christmas tree is full of surprises."

"I will," said Oscar as he waved good-bye with his tail and continued his journey. Up and up. Around and around. The higher he climbed, the sweeter the sound of the tinkling bells. He brushed by candy canes and silvery tinsel . . .

. . . and twinkling lights! It was like another world!

"Yikes, a monster!" Oscar yelled. Who was that lizard with the huge head? But it was just his own reflection gazing back from a great, glass bulb. Two voices giggled from behind him.

"Look at the alligator," one of them said, slapping his knee. "He almost jumped out of his skin!"

Oscar swirled around to stare at the peculiar ornaments laughing at him . . . two little men in brightly colored clothes, one hanging by his coat and the other by his pointy hat.

"For your information, I'm not an alligator. I'm an iguana," he told them.

"Well, *I–gwana* wish you a merry Christmas!" They exploded into laughter.

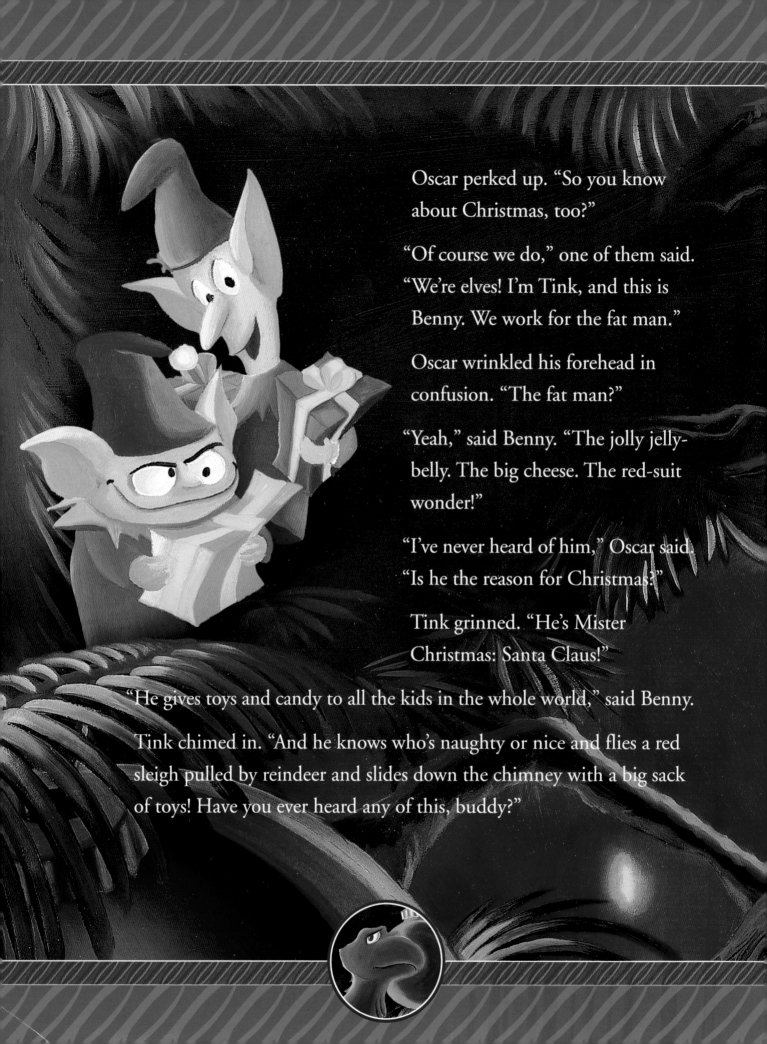

Oscar perked up. "So you know about Christmas, too?"

"Of course we do," one of them said. "We're elves! I'm Tink, and this is Benny. We work for the fat man."

Oscar wrinkled his forehead in confusion. "The fat man?"

"Yeah," said Benny. "The jolly jelly-belly. The big cheese. The red-suit wonder!"

"I've never heard of him," Oscar said. "Is he the reason for Christmas?"

Tink grinned. "He's Mister Christmas: Santa Claus!"

"He gives toys and candy to all the kids in the whole world," said Benny.

Tink chimed in. "And he knows who's naughty or nice and flies a red sleigh pulled by reindeer and slides down the chimney with a big sack of toys! Have you ever heard any of this, buddy?"

"No," said Oscar, shaking his scaly head. "So Christmas is a day to have parties . . . *and* get toys?"

"You got it!" said Tink. "It's all about toys. Why do you think people get so happy at Christmas? It's because of all the free stuff!"

Oscar wasn't too sure about this or about these elves either. But he politely thanked them and continued on his way.

Up and up. Around and around. Through the next row of branches, he could see an odd-shaped ornament made of felt and glitter and Popsicle sticks. It looked old. Across the front was written "1964."

"Hello," said Oscar.

"Hello," replied the shy ornament sweetly. "Are you lost? Can I help you?"

"Maybe. . . . Say, you don't look like the other ornaments on the tree," observed Oscar.

"I'm a keepsake," she said proudly. "I was made with love and care by Charlie's father when he was a little boy. See?"

"Wow, you are old," said Oscar. "You must be wise. Can you tell me what Christmas is all about?"

The Keepsake smiled. "Christmas is about families and people helping other people. They give food to needy children. They take blankets and clothes to homeless people, and they donate money to churches."

1964

Oscar was really dizzy now. "But I thought everybody had parties and got free toys at Christmas?"

"Oh, no," Keepsake replied. "Christmas is a time for being with your family and helping others. I've been around for many years, and I've seen the joy that it brings."

That's strange, Oscar thought. *Imagine people who would help others only at Christmas. Why not all the time?* But he kept this to himself and waved good-bye with his tail.

"Be careful!" Keepsake called after him. "You're very near the top!"

So up and up, and around and around he went. *I wonder what lucky ornament sits way up here?* Oscar thought.

Oscar peered down through the branches. It was like sitting on a mountaintop! For the first time, Oscar could see almost the entire house—the living room, the kitchen, the playroom, and his cage in the corner. It looked so small!

Then at the very tip-top, Oscar met the most important ornament of all . . .

. . . a beautiful angel! Her porcelain face glowed, and her smile was so bright, it almost blinded him.

"Wow," Oscar said, suddenly timid. "You're the prettiest thing I've ever seen. No wonder they put you on top!"

"I'm an angel," she said. "A messenger of God. Angels brought the Good News to everyone on the first Christmas."

Oscar's face lit up with excitement! "You mean, you know the real reason for Christmas?"

The angel smiled. "It's all about a baby."

Now Oscar was so confused that his scaly, little head hurt.

"The Nutcracker said Christmas is for parties," he said, "for eating, singing, and dancing.

"Benny and Tink told me it's for getting toys from Santa Claus.

"And the Keepsake told me it's all about families and helping the needy and poor. Now you tell me it's about a baby! How can Christmas be all of those things?"

"Those things help us celebrate," said the angel, "but they aren't the reason for Christmas. The reason isn't even here on this tree. Look over there." The angel pointed across the living room to a tiny barn set high on the mantel above the fireplace.

Oscar never would have seen it if he hadn't climbed up so high! Inside the barn were tiny figures of people and animals . . . and in the center of them all was a baby.

"God sent His Son from Heaven for all of us. The baby's name
is Jesus, and He was born in a stable like that one, long ago.
Jesus is the reason for Christmas, Oscar. It's His birthday."

"A birthday for baby Jesus!" Oscar exclaimed. "That's why we sing and eat and give toys and presents and help each other?"

"That's right," the angel said, smiling. "And the best way to celebrate Christmas is by remembering Jesus and loving others the way He loves you."

"Say! My birthday is around Christmastime," said Oscar. "I guess that makes me a Christmas lizard!"

"That it does," agreed the angel. So she tied a red ribbon around his neck as a gift.

"Now it's time for you to go back home," she said.

Oscar looked down and gulped. "I don't know. . ."

"Don't worry, Oscar," the angel said. "I'll help you." She hugged Oscar tightly and spread her wings.

Lifting off the treetop, they glided through the air! Down they flew, past all of Oscar's new friends. The Nutcracker gave a snappy salute, Keepsake waved good-bye, and the elves bounced on branches as they cheered for the flight.

They flew past the tiny manger scene with the smiling baby inside. Christmas! What a wonderful time . . . and filled with so many wonderful things!

They touched down gently. Oscar thanked the angel as he slipped inside his cage, and she flew back to the top of the tree.

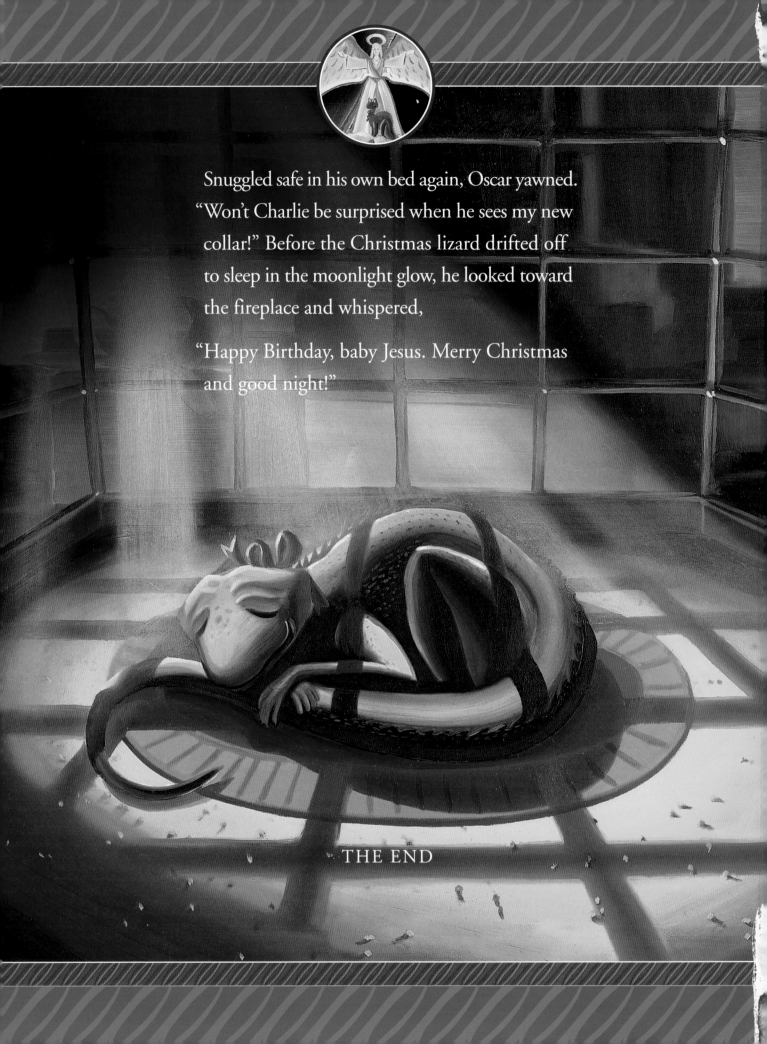

Snuggled safe in his own bed again, Oscar yawned. "Won't Charlie be surprised when he sees my new collar!" Before the Christmas lizard drifted off to sleep in the moonlight glow, he looked toward the fireplace and whispered,

"Happy Birthday, baby Jesus. Merry Christmas and good night!"

THE END